Statistically Speaking "From A Black Girls Perspective"

Sakevia Wilder

The content contained within this book may not be reproduced, duplicated, or transmitted without direct written permission from the author or the publisher.

Under any circumstances will any blame or legal responsibility be held against the publisher or author for any damages repartition or monetary loss due to the information contained within this book either directly or indirectly.

Legal Notice:
This book is copyrighted and protected. It is only for personal use. You may not amend, distribute, sell, use, quotes or phrases at any part, or the content within this book without the consent of the author or publisher.

Disclaimer Notice:
Please note the information contained within this book is for educational use and author verse of her life story purposes only all effect has been excluded to present accurate up-to-date reliable and complete information. No warranties of any kind are declared or implied. Readers acknowledge that the author is not engaged in the rendering of legal, financial, medical, or professional advice. The content within this book has been derived from life experiences and various sources.

Copyright © 2024-All rights reserved.

ISBN: 978-1-7355190-4-3

Written by Sakevia Wilder

Layout by Space 2 Launch Inc.

All rights reserved.

Published by Space 2 Launch Inc.

Statistically Speaking "From A Black Girls Perspective" and associated photos, logos, trademarks, and design elements are registered, owned, and licensed by Sakevia Wilder.

No part of this publication may be reproduced, stored in a retrieval system, or transmitted in any form or by any means, electronic, mechanical, photocopying, recording, or otherwise without written permission of the publisher or author.

Space 2 Launch Publishing Inc.
space2launch@gmail.com
954-464-3134

Dedication

This book is dedicated to my grandmother, who loved me unconditionally, saved me with her prayers, and took me in repeatedly, my heart and guardian, Angel Estella "Tiny" Curry.

> "Keke' you catch more flies with honey than you do vinegar."
>
> **—Grandma Tiny**

This book inspires and shows young girls and women that life has hidden valleys, back alleys, mountains, caves and even deep pits, but they are also disguised as obstacles, trials and tribulations. We either go through them or get over them to get to the other side of what life offers us.

There is indeed no testimony without a test, and we are all walking and breathing testimonies. We must be grateful for all that we have endured and all we had to GROW through because we would not be who we are today without them and the guidance of God.

Table of Contents

Dedication iv
Introduction 1
Generational Trauma 2
Mother & Daughter 7
Father & Daughter 14
The Runaway 20
Sexually Active 32
Self-Sabotage 39
Ugly 42
A Product of Society 46
The Product of the 80's The Felicia Ann Smith Story 49
Conclusion 53

Introduction

From the time I could remember, I have always felt alone, and unwanted love was looked for in my life by some man throughout my childhood and even adulthood.

This book tells a story about how sex ruled my life and how searching for impactful love landed me in one of the most identity crises ever. I will open up about my relationship with my parents, how sex became a reason to live, how I searched for love and never found it, how my insecurities took hold of me and completely led me to self-hate, bitterness, rebellion, and prostitution at the age of 16; and many other things amongst these trials as well as overcoming many steps in my life and on how I became a statistic to society, but what also defined my life and made me change and the reason "I am Statistically Speaking "from Black Girls Perspective."

Generational Trauma

From the time I can remember, sexual activity has always been a part of my life, and in my family, it was okay if you did not tell anyone or get caught. I grew up thinking that you were supposed to be touched, which was a way of showing love. I used to get seen in some form of sexual act with a younger family member or friend; no matter where I went, I was constantly being sexual before I knew what it was to be that way.

The first time I got caught, I was about five or six, and I was playing house with my boy cousin, and all I could remember was the feeling of being loved and cared for, just like couples feel. I believed in my little mind that I was supposed to find love, perhaps at five. I used to get caught so much that my mom separated me from the other kids.

It all started when I was the impressionable young age of 5. My mom gave me the privilege of going to my cousin's house, and one of my girl cousins would suggest we playhouse there. From that day onwards, we played the silly game and stayed that way for about a year. We did it so often that it became common among us, and all my cousins joined. Now thinking about it, I could not be mad at her because that was all she knew.

   I grew up hearing stories of my family members being raped and molested and having relationships and even babies. I'm unsure if it is true, but I have seen some things I know. Some men in our family are manipulating, sneaky, in what was supposed to be a close, loving family. I remember one of my family members being outside on a scorching day fixing one of my aunt's houses, and he was out telling me and my older cousins that it was okay for our male family members to touch us even if we didn't want them to.

   I believed it for a while until I got older and realized that was not the right thing to do. That same family member touched me a few times later when I was older. I didn't complain because I was so into him and thought he was my boyfriend. I remember this day like it was yesterday, my mom trusted him to watch me and my brother. He sent my brother to his room, and he had nothing on him except his boxers. His king size mattress sat in the middle of his living room, his sheets and pillows cascading across the bed. I could still smell his cologne as if he were sitting beside me. I remember seeing his penis hanging out of his boxers as he lay in the middle of the bed and said to me, "Keke," come sit on my lap holding his hands out for me as if I were a toddler that wanted to be held. So, I came over and sat on his lap while he lay there with a smirk showing his chipped gold teeth. He giggled and said, "You're so grown now." He then began to position my little body as I sat on him so that I would then straddle him. I looked him in his eyes and smiled because, in my premature mind, I finally had a boyfriend. I did not care how close in the family he was, I did exactly what he asked, but then I heard a knock on the door. He threw me off of him so fast and screamed in a panic, get up! But I, unaware of what could happen if he got caught, went into the room with my younger brother. When he finally opened the door, I heard it was his girlfriend at that time who came to take us out. I remember walking out the door before the family member, and I told his girlfriend that her boyfriend was now my boyfriend. She had a shocked look on her face, unsure of what I meant. She replied with a confused look and said, "What? I just said nothing and walked away to get in the car.

It was so bad for me that everywhere I went, I would pick out some boy in the room and kiss or touch him exposing them to what I was accustomed to. I was labeled Grown and fast as hell to everybody I came across, and there was a time when I would think about a relationship with a boy who would take care of me and love me. I was "hunching" everybody because that is all I adapted to. I would get caught up with a girl or anybody I felt liked me all before I was ten. As I got older, I always wondered why I was like this and why my family was this way.

This behavior followed me into my teens and even into adulthood. I found that I relied on sex to help me cypher out love, not knowing I was going about it wrongly. I would hear new stories of all the kids being touched by a family member or two. I have always felt my family was sexually driven and sick, but the stuff I heard was disturbing. As I kept gathering information, I realized this had been happening for generations. Then it all made sense to me when I got confirmation of what was happening, and I was told that I would be the one to break that generational curse and that it would no longer be on my family anymore. I was filled with so much relief because I knew, as a mother, I would never want that unruly behavior performed on my children. There is no way or reason children should have to go through that. It is not mentally healthy for a child, especially in adolescence.

In my research, 3 out of 5 children are sexually molested and/or raped by a family member or friend and are pregnant by age fourteen. Often, we do not realize how traumatic the experiences have been to us. We don't even notice how much we limit ourselves and our thinking process. It holds us down mentally while delaying us from growing and moving forward to what can happen. Instead, we tend to focus on what happened to us, and in some cases, we keep it going and only do what we are accustomed to rather than overcoming our circumstances. I am here to tell you that you are not alone in any way. No matter what they say, it is not okay in any form. It is never too late to speak up about it to that person or someone else you can relate to or help; this must stop, and you can stop it. We all have traumas and triggers, and this is generational trauma. I had to realize that it was also generational habits I had to break from childhood. We have all been victimized and affected by this somehow, but it is up to you to forgive those who hurt you, forgive yourself, and let go so that you can flourish.

Mother & Daughter

I have always thought mothers and daughters were supposed to become best friends. I thought you were supposed to be close and look up to your mother. Your mother would be your role model, especially for young Black daughters.

Growing up, I was never close to my mom ever since I could remember. I always felt a distance between her and I, and now thinking back, although I was terrible and grown as all outdoors, I did what I wanted when I wanted, I respected my mother only because she was a force, and that force was not scared to beat me and embarrass the hell out me any time she got the chance as soon as I got out of line. My mom had me at eighteen and walked across the stage with me in her belly. I am the first of three, and even then, I realized I never felt a bond with my mom at three or four. I would always be with my grandmother. I would sleep with her, bathe with her, and go fishing. It got to a point where being with my mom felt awkward when my grandmother was not around. I remember not even wanting her to touch me.

I also remember arguments that would take place between my grandmother, letting me do whatever I wanted because I could do no wrong in her eyes and continually picking on my brother. It was so bad my mom and grandmother looked like they were coming to blows, and my grandmother moved out that day.

That same day after the argument, my mom walked down the street. I had no idea where she was going, and when I caught up with her, she said, "GO BACK WITH YOUR GRANDMA," loudly as she was upset with the meanest look on her face. I stayed because I knew she was mad at me. Still, I never knew how to express myself and especially to her. I will not make it seem like I was a saint or one of the good kids because I wasn't. I would steal, fight, and get suspended all by the time I was in fourth grade, letting boys touch me, being disrespectful, and not caring about me getting disciplined because it was customary by then. There was a time I made my mom so mad. She threw my baby sister's walker at me and beat me so bad I ran to the neighbor's house. I did some of the dumbest stuff, which was not called for. Maybe my mom was tired, and yes, I agree I should have gotten disciplined, but I don't think it should have been to that extent. However, the beatings were traumatizing. They really scared me and made an actual rebellion against her. I was 12 years old, and in my first year in middle school, I met this boy in my neighborhood. I was so happy that somebody liked me. I didn't notice his friend was stealing all my mom's expensive stuff out of her room because I was so busy trying to feel loved I didn't care when my mom found out. She was so upset with me and my brother that she stopped giving us Christmas presents for years.

    Now I admit I have not been the best daughter, and I resented her because I felt she never loved me, especially when she had my sister. It was something about their relationship that made me jealous and bitter I always thought that my baby sister was the daughter she always wanted I often compared myself to that baby, in some weird way I wanted to be her she was lighter in complexion, long beautiful hair and spoiled, something I would only dream of at the time. I felt real love whenever they bonded, and even to this day, I yearn for a connection like theirs. I used to hear all the time how people in my family hated how my mom treated me, and I thought of living in the world of my sister. I wanted people to see her as evil and believe me because I felt so alone, but they didn't know I had lost all privileges long ago. I put her through so much. My mom always justified her wrongs, but some days she was right even if she was dead wrong. I had put my mom through some of the dumbest situations and put myself in predicaments I had no business in, like murder investigations, running away, going to jail, skipping school, sneaking boys into our home, stealing, and fighting in department stores. Still, nothing compares to December 25, 2011. At this time, I was sixteen, and I already had my son. Of course, I was bitter because I didn't get anything for Christmas, but my mom offered to take my son for a while. I was with one of my favorite mentors, whom I felt was like a mother to me. She listened to me and even bought me gifts, I was late returning to get my son from my mom, and she was so angry at me.

 I remember her confronting me and her and I exchanging vulgar words, hitting me in the street, in front of my mentor, and that's when I thought to myself that this "BITCH" doesn't like me, she is always embarrassing me, and I didn't do anything, and this time I did nothing wrong. So, being that rebellious little girl, I hit her back, and we were fighting like two pit bulls, fighting like two strangers on the street. I remember that fight vividly, feeling the hate and being fed up with every blow we gave each other. To be honest, that may be one of the times we bonded. I know it sounds insanely crazy, but at this time, I grew to hate her. I always felt she did some of the worst things to me and justified them. I was so tired of everything. I remember spitting in her face, picking up my sister's purple Hannah Montana skateboard, and hitting her on the head with every hateful bone in my body. That made me realize my strengths and created a dark place in my heart for her. My hate for her grew so much that I didn't care if she lived or died. I was happy seeing her being mistreated or going through some ugly situation. It made me evil and cold-hearted. I harvested this strong hate for her, and now I will say this, thinking back, "My mom did not deserve some of the things I did or said to her." I am not justifying it, but that was the only way she would talk to me. I believe all mothers have a phrase. Hers was to me when I did something stupid, she would say, "You wonder why I don't fuck with you because you always do dumb shit." But by the time I was a teenager, I did not care if she fucked with me or not because I was already fending for myself.

    My mom loved me and cared even after all the messed-up stuff with our relationship. She tried to help me, even put me in a home for girls with behavioral issues and put locks on the doors and windows so I wouldn't run away. I even remember her trying to pray with me. In fact, she tried so hard, but at that time, it was already too late. My demons were already too strong. I had experienced my first love and had sex. It was over, thinking back so much that had transpired between us; from her not wanting me to be around and me being stubborn and not respecting authority. There was nothing else left to do but fight, so that Christmas night, I felt that was the only time I was seen, but of course, that did nothing but make things worse. So many years later, my mom and I did not get along, but I will tell you this: whenever something transpired, she was there, and she always helped me with my kids no matter what. She probably couldn't stand me but that was all I had between her and my grandmother.

Later, I discovered that she felt her parenting wasn't the best, but she tried. She said how she raised us was like how she was raised and that when she had me and my brother, she was still learning and raising herself. With that, I learned as a mother that you must be patient with your kids. However, there are always alternatives to discipline and raise your child. The relationship between me and my mom still needs work, but I felt it was necessary to love and respect her from a distance and maintain my well-being like I have been doing since I was sixteen. In my research, eight out of ten teenagers have full-out brawls, and relationship issues are known and unknown. Still, I want you to know that we only have one mother, and no matter the circumstances, we are to respect and honor them even if they use their authority against us. We must remain humble and let it all play out in divine time; everything will run its course. There is nothing like a mother's love!

Father & Daughter

In my research, single-family homes are common in minority communities and only consist of a mother. Over 11 million families with children under 18 are fatherless, living with their mothers.

As you know, I was raised by my mother, and our relationship was not healthy, but to help you understand some of my issues, I wish to be as transparent as possible. My impactful memories with my father are just a few, but they are still vivid and memorable good and bad. My first memory of my father was when I was about four, and one of our family friends lived down the street from him. While I don't know what drove my parents to split, I see that it was a stale feeling when they were around each other. My mom called me to her and said come with me. I remember walking up to these large bushes on a pitch-black night. I saw this dark-skinned man just standing there. My mom stopped me in my track and said do you know who that is. I looked up and said no; she said with so much excitement that's your daddy.

At that time, I was thinking Daddy. 'What Daddy?' It felt like I never even heard daddy or knew what that was. I remembered saying hi and being still. From then on, I rarely saw him, his mom, my grandmother would come and pick me up and take me to a few places, and I would remember not knowing who my mom would send me with and just being quiet all the time. I would never be with him because he would always be on the go. We had never been to a party or even a walk around the block, maybe because he was fighting his demons, but just like my mom, I had no relationship with him. Not until I was older would I pop up to his house and say hi and maybe ask for money and occasionally get my hair done, but that was it. I was grateful for that, but I needed more, I needed his presence consistently. I yearned for his attention and unconditional love, I used to wish he would spoil me like I saw my sister get spoiled and loved, I remember being about sixteen and already on rocks with my mother. I looked to him for understanding. Now I admit I was in some way checking him for not being there for me, trying to have a conversation with him, while I was being demanding and disrespectful, He boldly said, 'YOU BETTER WATCH WHO YOU ARE TALKING TOO,' and let me explain this to you. When your mama got pregnant with you, I gave her money for an abortion. She said, "No, I'm keeping my baby, and that let me know right then and there that you were her baby and that all I had to do was pay child support, and that's what I have been doing, and I just looked at him in disbelief while my eyes watered and I said that's all you feel you need to do that's foul and I just remember crying in my aunt's arms as I was leaving and just walking away mad, not trying to resolve it thinking just let it die, I would eventually pop back up years after.

One of the most impactful and damaging times I would ever have to reflect on is Memorial Day, 2014. My aunt invited me to a barbeque for my cousin's birthday with my kids. The kids were in the pool playing, and everybody was lounging and hanging out. I walked over to my dad with a little smirk now. I have a slick mouth, and as I said before, I am not an angel, and I could be disrespectful, but, in just that moment, I remember standing next to my aunt's old Honda next to my dad and at that time, I always called him father. He said, I'm always going to call you 'Greasy' since you always call me father, because you always look greasy, now being that he does not really know me I knew he wouldn't know how sensitive I was about my looks, and I would never have thought he would comment on them rather it being true or not because didn't know my past trauma. At that moment, I brought up his lifestyle and child support in that same sentence, 'Now You' know you cannot bring up child support to a black man, and I saw his face turn up and say you want to talk about child support, but I have more money than you and knowing what I knew, I said, yea, sure, you have more money than me but do you have papers to show how got that money? He sucks his teeth and says let me tell you something, and I quote, "I never wanted you. Your mama should have swallowed you like the rest of your brothers and sisters." I was speechless, so I walked away very embarrassed and he followed me and he said it again even louder and everybody stopped and starred he walks in my face and I through my keys on my car and I mumbled I'm about to punch him in his shit at this time we were face to face I could smell the Heineken on his breathe and I thought to myself why would I respect this man I barely know him I think I should let him know what a monster I could be I just cocked back and punched him in the face a few times we tussled like two strangers in the street and we went to fighting like two rivals who hated each other my older brother on my dad side came to break it up and yelled to everybody "y'all just going to let her keep hitting him", I was furious he not only did it out in the open he did it front of my two sons I was so embarrassed I was in the middle of the street cursing and crying and my father said don't come around here anymore, you're not my daughter, I sank in disbelief and hurt all I wanted was a father I already felt like my mother quit on me now my dad this was a feeling no young girl should ever feel and words no young girl should ever hear, Then what made it worst is when his mother came out and said well Keke he had never been there for you just don't come over here anymore, just leave I couldn't believe it all I could say is how could you say that and why. Do you remember the bush told you I first met him? Well, that's the same bus I punched him in the face at that time. I felt justified and it's never okay to hit your parents. I felt like having a father would have played a significant role in my life. I thought I would have structure, love and respect. I probably wouldn't have kids if I had that real daddy-daughter relationship because he would be my first love.

Statistics show children without fathers turn to robbery, some form of criminal act, drug use, and more.

I fell into sex because I had major daddy issues and was looking for a piece of my father in each of these men. It is essential to instill structure and give guidance to a child. Having a father and/or father figure is very important, as is having active and positive parents. I'm sharing my stories with you, so you know why some of these things I did impact my life tremendously. I want you to know that if you are going through this situation or something similar, these things are meant to make you a better person and not break you down. I thank my father and especially my mother because if I didn't go through that trial with them, I would never understand their value in my life or what it's like to go as hard as I do. After all, I believe I am the black sheep in this situation. But as I said, remain humble and still respect your parents because the reward for you prevails and shows them that the situation you were in with them did not break you or define you. All I ever wanted from my father was honest love, guidance, and time. These are qualities I looked for all my life in men, especially older men, and this changed my outlook on what love could be for me, and that was even when I fought my mom and now my dad, the only person I had left was myself, and I knew I wasn't going to leave me, so I then learned to love myself, spend time with myself and count on myself in the end I won't let me down.

    My parents are who they are, flaws and all, but because they are who they are, I am who I am.

The Runaway

Parents could be rough, scary, strict, abusive, and all those things as kids make us furious and ready to leave home or runway and do not care where we end up if it is not with our parents or guardians.

Runaways, including boys, often are subject to violent gang-related activities, including sex trafficking, prostitution, rape, and suicide.

The first time I ran away, I was twelve years old, and even then, I was having trouble with my mom. I would steal her clothes to wear to school, steal her jewelry and shoes, and go to school to be more popular and get the attention I wanted. Now my brother and I would steal her things and take them to school, but this time was one of the most hurtful days I had ever experienced. I was home like usual on this day while my mom headed out. Then we had time to do what we wanted, break into somebody's home, go swimming, and have a boy or company over because my mom was never home. Still, on this day she was leaving, and she and her boyfriend at the time had his kids in the car. She called to me, "Keke," go get my iPod out of the room.

I ran and got it. When she got it from me, she looked at the cord and saw it was broken, and she asked what happened to my earphones and I said I don't know, now I admit I have stolen her iPod before but every time I stole it I put it back in good shape. I remember this look on her face in disgust and dislike. I was holding a CD player that I had gotten from Toys for Tots, and that was the only thing I got for Christmas that I was using besides the checkers set her boyfriend bought me that he secretly brought because my mom didn't want anyone buying me anything because I didn't deserve it after I let those boys steal all her things. So, she asked for the CD player and threw it in front of everybody outside and smashed my CD player on the concrete, I could still hear the broken pieces hitting the ground as she walked to get into the car. I cried and cried. I was so hurt knowing I did not break her iPod cord I went into the house upset. I was so broken that I laid on the couch in my brother's room and kicked the wall so hard that I put a hole into it. I was so scared of getting into more trouble. I thought that if she destroyed my CD player, imagine what she'd do to me. So, I started packing a suitcase with my clothes and left the house, not knowing where I was going. Still, I knew I had to get the hell away from that house, so I packed a bag, walked, and walked until I saw anything that looked familiar. I ended up at my elementary school and saw one of my classmates that lived nearby playing outside with the neighborhood kids. I ran over and played.

I rode a bike up and down the street. I even tried to get my classmate to convince her mom to let me spend the night. Until I saw a police car patrolling the area, and I said let me go. The police are searching for me. I tried to get away on the bike. Thinking back, it was funny now because I was joking until I rode the bike to a dead end, and the police officer stopped me and said where you are going. I said to my cousin's house, and he said are you sure and turned around at his computer desk and went well, who is this and pointed at the picture of me on the stand and smirked at me. All I could remember saying was, damn and thinking she really sent for me, that officer took me back home. I saw my mom's face. I remember her taking me with her to get her hair done to keep an eye on me. We still didn't talk about it, I always felt maybe that's one of the reasons I grew so much hate for her because we never really spoke unless she was screaming or talking at me, and that never made a possible impact. I think disrespect grew with time.

You see, I was so desperate for love I did not care who you were; I needed you to spend real time with me, even if you wanted to touch me sexually. Now the second time I ran away, I was still twelve, and that night I snuck in some neighborhood boy. He was trying desperately to be my first when my little brother ran and told my grandmother what I was doing in the washroom. I remember her coming to the washroom saying what do you have to show me, boy? and when she turned the corner, she started hitting the boy, yelling get the hell out of my house and saying Keke, what are you doing? I kept saying, please don't tell my mom crying, but I knew she was. So, I fell out the back door on a cold Sunday night walking in the dark, only wearing a shirt, boxers, and a pair of socks. I roamed the streets for a while, not knowing where to go, so the first place I went to was the i95 Bridge on Pembroke Road. I walked under the bridge, sat at the top, and just sat for a minute while I listened to the cars pass by and roar under the passageway.

When I arrived at the bridge, I thought there would be other people there that would welcome me, love me, and show me the way of life under that bridge. But it was just me alone, so I decided to keep walking. I ran across moving cars until I reached my middle school, McNicol Middle school, where I walked around the school and talked to myself, imagining a better life. It was so nippy outside that I picked up an old jacket one of the kids at the school left. I put it on and walked some more until I walked to the park at the after-school campus and played on the prickly hard plastic grass I covered myself with the jacket I found until it got too cold to stand. I walked across the street to the pay phone and called the police so that they could take me anywhere but home. I was so terrified of seeing my mom. I would rather sleep in the park, so I ran back to the little park, played in the playground, and saw the police pass by, and I slept there until I heard the bell ring for school. By that time, it was early morning, and the sun was out. I was hungry and barely clothed. I sat and watched the ESE students come out for PE as I eased up little by little, so anxious to be seen. I remember a little person who was a teacher's aide stopped me and said young lady came here, and he walked me to the office, where they called my mom and grandmother to get me.

I was lucky the first two times because to be honest I didn't stop running away then I ran away so much it wasn't even running a way anymore I would leave but being an adult now I noticed I ran away from my problems I never faced what was in front of me I would always run but then I was also the type to get what I wanted and take whatever came my way and now realizing I always felt like I would be better off in the streets and not at home where I had a bed, hot food, a roof over my head and all the necessity to live like a child, Until I a ran away for 2 weeks and right before my 13th birthday I remember coming home to an empty house nobody was there and I had no idea where they went the house was very empty the only thing in the house was a blanket and pillows that I used to cover up with after I ate this 2 week old steak that my mom had mistakenly left in the oven but even then I still didn't learn I just couldn't be home I was still searching for love and to answer your question from who I don't know. I remember a story that hit the news a few years ago where a young girl that I went to school with but was never affiliated with was murdered by one of our schoolmates after she ran away from home and was hidden and decaying behind a dumpster for weeks and thinking back, that could have been me and if you're reading this. You are in the streets; this could really be you. When we are young and so into ourselves and feel like authority is beneath us we risk a lot without even recognizing it we put ourselves in situation that we have no business being in, we go through stuff that could have been avoided if we would put are pride, issues and stubbornness to the side and just be a child in most cases we don't have to run away unless it's not healthy to be in the household, I remember sleeping in the park many nights getting bit by mosquitos, breaking into people cars at three in the morning and sleeping in them all because I would rather not be in the same house as my mother I chose to leave and run away from home instead of respecting authority rather it was abused authority I made a choice and I had to deal with the choices I made and my choice was to walk the streets from neighborhood to neighborhood walking from every hood Melrose, Parkway, Tater Town and other hoods at night looking for a boyfriend walking in abandoned houses not knowing what could happen to me, I almost got raped a couple times, I've been humiliated in all most every way possible all because I put myself in those positions and I'm grateful that's all that happen to me, I remember walking in Tater Town one night and this guy sees me and try's to talk to me and I asked him which way was De Lavoe park and he anxiously said I'll show you I'll walk you there and we walked there and I walked up the playground and sat down, now I'll remind you this was at 12:00 in the morning, I was so anxious to be out and explore what I thought was good for me, as I'm sitting the guy no more than 21 who was looking for some little girl like me to get his hands on and when he made his move I decline and left quickly, so I continued to sit and crouch my knees to my chest and fell asleep, when I woke up I awoke to somebody kicking me and when I opened my eyes I was surrounded by at least twenty young boys laughing and asking why am I sleeping in the park and yelled saying 'no I'm up', I was waiting for someone and some of those boys wasn't paying me any attention but some of them were and they were ready to get whatever I was offering or take it if necessary and so I started walking to leave the park as I'm walking away they started picking up rocks and throwing them in my direction, I was so terrified and worried on what could happen to me I had to speed walk I couldn't go anywhere to sleep. I didn't want to go home so as I made my way out of the boy gang but still followed me and walked behind until one of the older guys in the gang stood up for me and walked me home, and like I said I was not going to my mom's house so I made it seem like I lived at one of my mom's old boyfriend house and sat on the porch until I fell asleep and hours later his grandfather went outside to read his morning paper and woke me up to go in the house, I knew then that I had love but it didn't stop there I ran away for a few years more we don't realize the love people have for us until we don't have that love anymore people washed their hands with me all because I was not obeying my mother and being a child hell my own mother washed her hands with me and when I would run away she would lock the doors change the locks then sleep in living room in case I tried to sneak back in and when I would give in she wouldn't let me in that's when I would get smart I later learned that when you run away or get put out your parents or legal guardian can't put you out, so I would call the police on myself so my mom would let me in and it would work every time, but eventually it grew old.

My mother was so tired of it my room wasn't a room anymore I remember sleeping on the cold hard floor not being able to get in to my room or her friends having sex in my bed I would sneak in the windows and sleep in the closet, I remember one time she found me in the closet inside a shoe ben and put me back outside all that was on me I chose to make the bed and I had to live in it literally it got so bad I was so desperate to get back in the house I played like I was drunk in the drive way like somebody just laid me there and ran away like they did that guy on house party, I remember just lying in there with my eyes closed trying to seem unconscious and my mom and her friend looking at me crazy and hoping I wasn't dead, I remember them pouring water on me to wake me up bucket after bucket talking so much trash and all I wanted was for them to pick me up and put me in the house but that took a long time then, I knew my mom was fed up and tired of my recurring events, sometimes While we are in these phases it takes for our parents or whoever to give up on us for us to see what we had and what we miss to make us better, realize our strengths and fend for ourselves to see what we had was so good. I remember this one time I was gone for a while. I ran away once again and walked up and down the streets of Broward County. I went to a park called Saint George, where I slept. After hanging out all day, I would sleep on the park benches under the pavilions and wake up to the early-morning joggers walking the track. I was walking the streets, I was so tired, and desperately wanted to go home, but I knew I had no way in. I would be seen by men with cars stopping to talk to me, jumping into their vehicles, going with them because they could feed me and give me a place to sleep after we had acquainted.

This one night I was hanging out with some random park boys and it was getting late and every one was heading home one by one by this time it was one guy at the park sitting with me now I have always been surrounded by boys trying to persuade me to give them my virginity and even offering me hundreds of dollars at thirteen years old so it was normal to be around them and act like a home girl but this time I was all alone with this one boy or should I say man he was short, hazel eyes, light skin, long dreads, beard and a missing tooth in the front of his mouth we were casually talking until he grabbed me and pinned me to the wall by my neck and looked me dead in my eyes trying to take my pants off I was so scared but I kept a straight face and evil looking grin and said "boy get the fuck off me" he held me for a while until he just let me go and walked off I quickly ran to the other side of the park and slept under a pavilion where I could see if anyone was coming the next day I walked to the swap shop to steal clothes and eat I later walked back to the park and decided it was time to move to another park so then I began walking I saw this car pull up on the side of me real slow thinking it was a man I stopped but then I saw a familiar face it was one of my mom's child hood friends Arlette who made me get in her car and took me with her to her house and called my mom I did not want to go because I knew the consequences ahead but to be honest I was happy to be off my feet I was tired, hungry and dirty from not bathing properly for weeks of sink bathing thinking back I can't believe I put myself in those positions what Arlette didn't realize was she saved me because in my mind I was looking for someone to rob that same day I finally slept a comfortable sleep when I went to her house and I got ready to see my mother after speaking to her and trying to stay on track I went back to school and did what I called my best, after some time I saw this girl with a paper and on that paper was a registered sexual offender (rapist) he was light skin, long dreads light eyes and 5'2 I looked at the picture and it was the same guy who pinned me to the wall that one night at the park thinking back I could have been brutally raped and murdered all because I wanted to be in the streets looking for love but what I ultimately found was favor grace and mercy realizing as an adult it has been god protecting me, loving me and delivering me out of harm's way even though that was the route I chose he still detoured me to a better life and for that I am so thankful as well as grateful for the covering over my life and the people in it. If you resonate with this, take this time to reflect on your life and forgive yourself for whatever it is you put yourself through.

Reflect, Forgive, Shift

-Sakevia Wilder

Sexually Active

Apart from trying to help save someone by going through the same or similar situations you were experiencing; you must be honest with yourself and that person. Even if it's embarrassing, you must always be truthful to make that person not want to end up in the same situation and change for the better.

I have always had somebody lecture me and try to help me realize who I was, but it just did not take. We all need guidance and structure, no matter who we are. I remember being young and always dancing and at that time it being cute and funny to dance everywhere I go my mom encouraged at family functions I was always the winner at parties for dance contest and it that made me feel good that was the only time I was noticed, but when I got older all I wanted to do was to be seen and find a boyfriend but my self-esteem was shot. I was getting into all kinds of trouble it went from being cute to me being so damn grown and nobody wanting to watch me because I was 'So Grown'.

I remember one of my older family members sitting in the car. While my mom was in the store and just looking at me with the ugliest meanest look on her face in so much disgust and telling me how she did not like me because I was so grown. She can't stand my grown ass and that its sad I have no friends, and that I wouldn't be nothing in life she used to be so mean to me when my mom would be gone, and I would never tell her because I always felt she would never take up for me so every time that happened, I never said anything. That cousin made me feel even worse about myself and things worsened from there. I was desperate for love. I would let anybody touch me from then on. Whenever I would run away, I would find myself getting in cars with total strangers, old men, young guys, anybody willing to spend time with me. I used to wander the streets and doing so I experienced what happens when you do not comply. I got left in far places kicked out of cars amongst being humiliated, now I know I didn't have to be in those situations but I was I never complied until I met my first whom I thought was it for me little did I know that this was not it for me I remember sneaking in his window and having sex for the first time as I gazed at projector that said September 27, 2007 the day I lost my virginity now being that I was only thirteen and I was used to being touched I never had actual sex.

I remember not knowing what was going on to my body, but it was a feeling I couldn't explain, and I thought that having him do these things to me meant he was my boyfriend, until he got around his friends' while disclaiming me'. He would talk about me among them but always wanted to have sex with me. I was thirteen years old, and I thought having an eighteen-year-old boyfriend in my head was everything, every guy I encountered from then on was ten or twenty years older than me. "Yes, I'll say it" 'I HAD SERIOUS DADDY ISSUES.'

I would run away to be with any guy, and they didn't matter if I had to have sex, I just wanted to feel cared about and somewhat loved I just forced my way into the world with full warning I ignored it all I didn't care about a condom, who it was as long they looked presentable. By the time I was fourteen years old I had multiple STD's and sexual transmitted infections all at one time from having unprotected sex with Lord knows who and not to mention I was also pregnant all at the same time.

Now I will be honest I would experience things going on with my body and didn't know what to do I left it untouched and still had sex not knowing it would affect other people, myself, and my first-born son. At that time I ran away and stayed with my classmates mom who treated me like I was older and kind of let me do what I wanted and she told my mom for me and again I have to remain honest I still didn't understand what was going on I just knew I was pregnant and I was happy because I was going to be a mom and I was going to have a family, I had to get two shots in my thighs and take three different pills that felt like rocks going down my throat I really hadn't realize what happened and what I could have contracted, Aids, HIV, genital herpes amongst other disease that could've made me hemorrhage, make me sterile and have to remove my ovaries and maybe even my cervix, but I am thankful I could be cured and all I got to keep was a child I was five months pregnant and there was no telling how long I was carrying those disease before I found out I was carrying a baby, my baby was indeed affected by my carelessness. I took medication that was harmful to him and that led him to be mentally delayed by three years old. I thank my mother for stepping up and helping me after all I put her through with my unhealthy lifestyle. I look at my son today and feel bad because he struggles with learning and I know it is because of me, **we are humans who think of the now and not what could happen in the future instead of reflecting on what or who our actions will affect.**

Now that should have taught me and put me in my place with me pregnant and my diagnosis, but it didn't I moved back home with my mom went back talking to several guys and never told my mom who my child's father was by that time, I was fourteen years old pregnant and my child's father had moved on and still didn't know how old I was till I was seven months pregnant when he was twenty-three at the time my mother ended up telling him the whole truth even about my STD problems. That still made no impact after I had my son was still doing some of the senseless stuff leading me to be re-infected with more STD's having human papillomavirus scare at fifteen years old, by the time I was sixteen years old, I had already had sex with sixty-five different men that I kept count of and thought nothing of because I was still looking for someone to love me and to be loved by someone. It got even worse when I met this younger girl who was fourteen and introduced me to prostitution I was out of control and so uneducated about this lifestyle I put myself in really bad predicaments by that time my mom had really washed her hands with me I needed money to live and support my son I was stealing out of stores and boosting the products, prostituting and skipping school at sixteen I dropped out of middle school to pursue a career in prostitution I did what I wanted. I didn't care what my mom had to say because I felt she was already telling everything I did anyway. The rebellion was real. By the time I was seventeen, I was living with a customer whom I made believe I was in a relationship with and was wondering the world still while my mom took my son in as her own I later found out I would have another child with whom I had no idea and was so desperate for abortion I robbed and tricked to get it and never got a chance to get all of the money so I eventually moved back home a seventh grade pregnant drop out, horrible relationship with my mom no job just me and my unruly thoughts. So, I sought help and had my second son, and that's when life showed me who was 'Boss.'

I need you to please listen and reflect on this. I know you think that would never happen to me because I said the same thing. Women of color and even women of all races and men as well need to take care of our bodies and not take it for granite because we could put ourselves in life altering situations that could be deadly. **In my research, I have learned that one in four teens contract a sexually transmitted disease every year. This can be avoided with condoms and/or abstinence.** We must love the hell out of ourselves and respect our bodies and such, I do not regret anything I said or did because I needed to learn to change. I am one of those women and you could be to if you don't make a drastic change and for the women that have been in my exact or similar shoes you are not alone, I know it was rough, but we conquered the worst of things and believe it or not we have more to conquer rather it be mentally, physically or spiritually we always pull through and come out on top.

Self-Sabotage

By now it is not a secret I have experienced a war of love and self-hate for an exceptionally long time. I never thought I was beautiful and desirable to anybody. I forced myself on guys because I never felt real love. Somedays I would cry and did not know why. I tried my best to look presentable but every time I did, I would get humiliated and ridiculed on how I dressed myself by my family members and random people I would get in the most random fights just by walking on the street and someone commenting I'm ugly or being plain rude when they thought I couldn't hear them. I cared so much about what people said about me I remember trying to overdose on my grandmothers high blood pressure and cholesterol pills, I hated my life and self so much at a really young age, and felt I couldn't tell anybody because I was so terrified of my mom and the way she would discipline me, now of course I had behavioral issues but mentally it was more so on another level I just didn't care to say anything because nobody would help me. I have only admitted to a few people I was suicidal but when I took the knife and put it to my stomach I was done with even existing.

I remember having another episode with my mom after getting caught trying to rob her since I wasn't allowed in the house she caught me in the act red handed now thinking back on that situation I was really showing symptoms of drug use although I was not on drugs of any kind I was really acting like it in a way I was really seeking attention I did not know how to use my words and actually communicate and that made things even harder I was really trying to harm myself my mom ended up getting me baker acted I was in a place with real kids with real issues my problems were minor to there's I met kids who did drugs, cut themselves, hung themselves and even killed because they had real mental issues they were very unsure of themselves but found relief in using drugs or cutting themselves. I then came to a understanding after being in A insane place the way I acted out was a cry for help the only issues I had was because of me, I made things hard for myself I was my own poison I was self-sabotaging a life that could have been wonderful for me but instead I chose the streets that had no love for me and same the streets chewed me up and spit me out and little did I know I was making detrimental decisions and they did indeed affect my future. I was indeed my own saboteur my own worst enemy I was my own poison as well as my antidote and all I had to do was grow in to a better me, I changed my mind set and I gained whatever it was I lacked and I visualized a better version of myself once I did that realized my worth, A priceless individual with so much to offer the world.

Ugly

Unpleasant or repulsive, especially in appearance.

I was introduced to the word ugly when I was in my adolescent years when I was vulnerable and believed everything someone told me I remember being at a family event playing on the playground with some little girls I met, just being little kids and their mom and dad walked up and started to talk to them and to see if they were okay they then introduce me to their parents and their dad looked at me and said you are a ugly little thing I can't remember what I said but if you know me you know I said something real slick because then he said watch your mouth. The beginning of that was just a moment where a stranger helped me learn to hate myself. At that time, I valued the opinions of others and that led me to see what they saw when I was in middle school. I was picked on so much that the teachers and staff thought it was funny and from then I learned to defend myself. What if I told you I remember every person that ever called me ugly from as early as five till recently this year Growing up, I thought I looked good, but I was called ugly so much I just thought it had to be true. And I would think if different people said this all the time, then it's true. I heard it so much I started to pick on myself before anybody else could.

    Once I looked at myself in the mirror everything all those people said to me was true in my mind, I was burnt black crispy dirty gap teeth bald headed and just ugly I started to inspect myself I hated everything about me my dark skin, my nose, my big eyes the way I talked with my tongue the way my teeth never touched I just hated myself. But you would not know because I was always protecting myself with my anger. I would dare you to say something because I was always angry, unhappy, and insecure, fuel for a beast that had already been created inside of me, I was never afraid to fight or stand up for myself. But on the inside of my little mind. I wanted to be liked and accepted so badly by the girls at school I would steal my mom's perfume and shoes so that they would talk to me. I just really wanted to be seen by the boys but when the boy you have crushed on for a long time comes out and embarrasses you in front of the whole class and says the awful words all loud and aggressive eel she ugly after you told him that you like him it be little's you, it shatters your confidence I never believed I was beautiful as a child I don't care who said it I just knew that was not true I knew that nothing I did would change the way I looked as I got older I would like any boy/girl who I thought liked me I did not care I just wanted to be accepted ugly and all. Myself esteem was low, I had no confidence and I began to really hate my being in general but my motto was always "I'm ugly but I will beat your ass" and that stayed with me until adulthood I kept that mindset and used it as an excuse to make myself feel superior till this day I struggle with hearing those word but as an adult I know who I am I know what I am capable of and how I make me feel so the opinions of other don't make me how I value myself and love myself dose I am content with who I am an what I look like I embrace my beauty in side in out, and my personality alone will quiet the room. When I decided to love myself, I started noticing everything I was doing to make me hate myself. I remember comparing myself to other girls thinking that would make me happy if I looked like them or if I had what they had, that if I had those expensive shoes or perfume that I would get validation from anybody I wanted to be a part of a community that fed off my low self-esteem that made fun of the way spoke, the way I dressed and the way I looked to them. I then learned that some communities had no real values other than materialistic items and images. I lacked self-value. I was not worthy to even live. But as I got older and developed the meaning of self-worth and elevating my confidence in figuring out who I was wholeheartedly, I saw that how you look does not define who you are or your purpose in life.

You are the creator of your life here on earth and life is what you make it don't ever value someone else's opinion value yourself, motivate yourself, love yourself love validate yourself reflect in your life and do you self a favor and eliminate those limiting beliefs about yourself and who you are and what you are capable of doing, take this action for your life and watch your mindset change. To that same community I was seeking validation from thank you, thank you for helping me find myself and my purpose all though it has been a long dark depressing ride. I thank you for not accepting me for who I was then because you helped me grow and love myself and helped me become who I am today. Decide what kind of life you want and then say no to everything that is not that. My life is beautiful and so am I to those who judged me only made me better although I was criticized, I turned it all into positivity and remained humble while defining myself.

A Product of Society

Although my life has not been the best and I have endured hell and came out a winner. I got to keep my mind and stay true to who I am while taking those hard hits from life. I have been a deceiver, a thief, a teen mom, a runaway a prostitute, stripper and homeless while being per miscues, depressed and suicidal but I did not let that define me or decide how my life would turn out. Instead, I found myself loving myself. I let it build, mold me, and teach me. I am thankful for the life I had because it made me who I am and the peace of mind I have now is well worth everything I have ever lost; I was everything that the enemy said I was but nothing that the enemy thought I would become today. I am relentless, fearless, optimistic, worthy, and faithful and because of my demise I get to live and tell you the truth on overcoming being a statistic in the ghettos of America and therefore **'I AM STATICALLY SPEAKING'**.

We are all products of society rather it be a positive or negative impact. It has to do with your environment. We make decisions based on what we know and our background. We are the way we are because of our environment rather it be the way we speak, the way we a dress or even the way we think although there are ways to help better ourselves and change the environment we grew up in we sometimes get complacent with the life we have been dealt instead of changing the narrative it could be the world around us our friends and family depicting our lives all because we are to scared of what life really has to offer and place our limiting beliefs on others that wants change. Throughout life many people are going to tell you what they think is best for your life they all have their own opinions on what **YOU** should be doing or how **YOUR** lifestyle should be rather it be saving money, spending money doing drugs, not following your dreams but it is ultimately up to you to observe and be an independent thinker.

For example, growing up I thought public housing and government assistance was a normal thing to inherit. I thought it was something you were just given because everyone I knew around me was receiving it everyone was comfortable with being given pennies and living for a little to nothing instead of using the system as a stepping stone to save and obtain financial freedom and independence instead minorities would rather buy what they've always wanted rather than buy what they need and invest for what can carry us into our future we are all influenced by something or someone by whatever we choose to believe in we all have are differences but one thing we all have in common is the same 24 hours. To overcome our environment and our fears and obstacles. We are all given two things when we wake up: A chance and a choice and whatever you do with your chance is your choice. Although I was raised different from others I knew I wanted more out of life once I realized what was really going on I knew I wanted to be independent what we lack as people is knowledge and guidance as well as understanding I've learned to unlearn what it is I thought I knew and relearn and understand my surroundings and shift my mind set once I did that I saw the world different and I carried myself different and held my own self accountable for who I was becoming while keeping God first and when I did this I became limitless and a high valued product of society.

Every day we wake up its two things we get A chance and a choice. The choices that he makes after he get his chance is on him… that is on him he must live with that.

- J. Prince

The Product of the 80's
The Felicia Ann Smith Story

Growing up my mom would let me, and my younger brother go to my great aunt's house with my older cousins who would watch us while their grandmother went to work overnight. When I was younger I would always think my cousin were my great aunt kids because they would always call her by her nickname "Lillie Mae" they would never say grandma or nana, I remember never speaking much but always observing and the more I came over the more I noticed there mother was never around much I then came to notice the Lillie Mae was taking care of her four grandchildren on her own while working as an overnight radiologist in the local hospital in Miami Not until I got a little older did I start seeing my cousin's mother Lisa. Lisa was the only child of Lillie Mae; she had four kids, three girls and one boy at a young age and became addicted to crack in the mid 80's although I caught the tail end of it being born in 94, I observed Lisa I just knew something was wrong. As I got older Lisa would come around increasingly but what I did not notice was the more I saw Lisa the less I saw Lillie Mae.

Lillie Mae had gotten ill to the point she never went back to work so my grandmother and other aunt went searching all through the drug infested streets of Dade County looking for Lisa to come home to care for her pre-teen children at the time I recall going to Lillie Mae's house all the time until she passed away. By this time, my cousins were in high school, and I would rarely come over. Lisa was at the house more often because it was left to her, so she was then raising three children until they were court ordered into foster care and lost custody. Not shortly after, she later lost her mother's house. Now let me explain something to you about Lisa although she was on drugs Lisa was a very beautiful brown-skin women she was talented and could sing the roof of any building, I watched her try and mend her family with gifts dinners and even huge parties for her kids but she was secretly on drugs and wouldn't cooperate the way we all would hope the fight with drugs was a fight she just couldn't win in my opinion she was missing something in her life she felt drugs could help fill she was missing real love every time I would come over she had a new friend someone who made her feel good about herself and showed her the love she felt she needed until they would then betray her hearing some of the stories in my opinion she wanted love so badly it blinded her she chose many men over her kids and it destroyed that relationship with them.

Once she lost everything she turned back to the streets. She was on drugs even heavier, and the streets had gotten ahold of her and swallowed her whole. The Lisa I knew was beautiful, statues, talented, and strong but as the year passed on until my adult years that all faded. The last time I seen Lisa she was small could barely stand up straight she was frail, she was losing her hair couldn't walk as much and needed help using the bathroom her body was deteriorating from AIDS and it was bad between the drugs and the disease she was in a fight with life she had already lost the fight with her body and as I got to see her as we said our last goodbye to our beloved cousin Doletha at her funeral I got to spend time with Lisa I had to help her in and out of the tub and as I helped her I just reflected I looked back on my life and said to myself this can very well be me my cousin was suffering and it was nothing anyone could do about it. I worried for her all while being sick. She was homeless and staying in an abandoned crack house and would go missing to where her children would have to go looking for her until they just could not find her one day.

Felicia Ann Smith was found dead in one of those abandoned crack houses and labeled a jane doe no one in her family knew that she was dead until months later she was alone no family to bury her properly although she chose the street instead of fighting for a better life I always wondered what would happen if she used her talents or if she kept custody of her children how different everyone's life would be the way Lisa chose to go in her life impacted those that were close to her and often times we don't know what we've caused and how bad we have made it for others. Lisa's story is a daily reminder to persevere through every trial that comes your way, never to give up and put up one hell of a fight when life decides to knock you down. The crack epidemic in the eighty's still impacts our community four decades later, but I have learned that it is not what we went through. It's what we did to get out and jump over the fences of life that's what molds us for the better.

We are born like our parents, but we will die looking like our choices.

-Dale Bronner

Conclusion

She has been labeled a stripper, a teen mom, a runaway, and a seventh-grade dropout, but success was never one of them. Join Sakevia Wilder as she shares the chronicles of being a habitual statistic in society while being open and honest about all the experiences she grows through in life. While exploring and discovering who she was, finding her purpose and herself.

While becoming an adult and trying to adapt to what life offered me. I found myself moving up one step and going back five steps. My life was the scariest roller coaster I had ever ridden before then. The top drill dragster roller coaster, one of the world's most terrifying and deadly rollercoasters, had nothing on my life. The way I have been through loops, twist-back breakers, and near-death experiences, I surprise myself every day that I didn't give up even when I was close to the edge. I tried everything I could to try and get my life together. I listened to motivational speakers, read self-help books, and even changed my religion to better understand who I was. I would do whatever someone said if it meant a better me. I remember trying the two-cup manifestation method I learned on YouTube because I was at my breaking point and on the verge of suicide. Still, I realized I was doing it for the applause so people could see what I was doing so they could look at me differently in some way praise me.

    I always kept some income coming in, but I was doing just enough to stay above water. I was only reading to recite words; I never applied anything. I was doing what I felt I had to do instead of uncovering that there was more to life than the bare minimum. My life was a front I did nothing for a positive cause. It was simply to upstage my enemies. But then I noticed all the energy I put into this facade of a person I was being. I could educate myself, put in the work, and become who I knew I needed. I wanted success but didn't know how to get it. I then made up my mind, but I had to solve a couple of problems before I could go further. Although I read books and listened to many powerful speakers, I never changed. I never changed my mindset or how I was moving about life.

    I remember being broke, unhappy, bitter, jealous, and looking for someone to save me. I vowed never to enter these profound disgusting feelings again, so I came up with these five pillars to detour my life from the way it was once headed. After evaluating myself mentally, physically, and spiritually, I began to dive into my problems. I identified as weak, purposeless, a serial taker, and not holding myself accountable for my actions and decisions. I also realized I didn't know who I was and that it was something holding me back from my future FORGIVENESS. Once I organically connected with myself after working on myself, I saw that I was limitless after feeling limited for a very long time. Here are my five pillars to a stronger, healed, and prosperous you; Isolate, Reflect, let go, praise, Mindset shift, visualize.

-Sakevia Wilder

(ISSOLATE)

GET ALONE, SPEND TIME WITH YOU
GET TO KNOW YOURSELF
TAKE ACCOUNTABILITY FOR YOUR ACTIONS
MANAGE YOUR INSECURITIES
PRAY/MEDITATE

-Sakevia

(REFLECT)

CONFRONT YOUR FEARS

CRY AND OR LAUGH AT YOUR PAST (get it out)

FORGIVE YOURSELF FOR EVERY SINGLE THING YOU HAVE BEEN THROUGH

(PRAISE)

APPRECIATE YOU
SPEAK LIFE
PRAISE YOURSELF
THANK YOURSELF
REWARD YOURSELF

(LET GO)

FORGIVE THOSE WHO HURT YOU
ACKNOWLEDGE NEVER GIVING UP
MENATLLY HEAL

(MINDSET SHIFT)

REMOVE LIMITED BELIEFS
PUSH YOURSELF/GET TO KNOW YOUR STRENGTHS
FIND YOUR PURPOSE/CREATE
THINK ABOUT THE FUTURE
CHANGE YOUR ROUTINE
REMOVE WHAT YOU BELIEVE HENDERS YOU
SERVE OTHERS

(VISUALIZE)

WORK

SEE YOURSELF WHERE YOU WANT TO BE

WRITE THE VISION MAKE IT PLAIN

WORK

Statistically Speaking
"From A Black Girls Perspective"
Reflection

| What about the book inspires you? |

Statistically Speaking
"From A Black Girls Perspective"
Reflection

How can you relate to Sakevia?

Statistically Speaking
"From A Black Girls Perspective"
Reflection

What steps can you take to evolve mentally?

Statistically Speaking
"From A Black Girls Perspective"
Reflection

How important is it for you to forgive the ones who hurt you?

Statistically Speaking
"From A Black Girls Perspective"
Reflection

What are your views on mother & daughter relationships?

Statistically Speaking
"From A Black Girls Perspective"
Reflection

Write a letter to someone you've had differences with and let go.

Statistically Speaking
"From A Black Girls Perspective"
Reflection

What Triggers your Trauma? (Good or Bad)

www.ingramcontent.com/pod-product-compliance
Lightning Source LLC
Chambersburg PA
CBHW061740070526
44585CB00024B/2756